Purchased with Smart Start Funds

A NOTE TO PARENTS

When your children are ready to "step into reading," giving them the right books is as crucial as giving them the right food to eat. **Step into Reading Books** present exciting stories and information reinforced with lively, colorful illustrations that make learning to read fun, satisfying, and worthwhile. They are priced so that acquiring an entire library of them is affordable. And they are beginning readers with a difference—they're written on five levels.

Early Step into Reading Books are designed for brand-new readers, with large type and only one or two lines of very simple text per page. **Step 1 Books** feature the same easy-to-read type as the Early Step into Reading Books, but with more words per page. **Step 2 Books** are both longer and slightly more difficult, while **Step 3 Books** introduce readers to paragraphs and fully developed plot lines. **Step 4 Books** offer exciting nonfiction for the increasingly independent reader.

The grade levels assigned to the five steps—preschool through kindergarten for the Early Books, preschool through grade 1 for Step 1, grades 1 through 3 for Step 2, grades 2 through 3 for Step 3, and grades 2 through 4 for Step 4—are intended only as guides. Some children move through all five steps very rapidly; others climb the steps over a period of several years. Either way, these books will help your child "step into reading" in style!

For Corey, David, and Brian
—S.K.

To those who always inspire my bones:
Taylre, Aubry, Whitney, Camry and Mason
—D.J.

Text copyright © 1999 by Stephen Krensky. Illustrations copyright © 1999 by Davy Jones. All rights reserved under International and Pan-American Copyright Conventions. Published in the United States by Random House, Inc., New York, and simultaneously in Canada by Random House of Canada Limited, Toronto.

www.randomhouse.com/kids

Library of Congress Cataloging-in-Publication Data
Krensky, Stephen.
Bones / by Stephen Krensky ; illustrated by Davy Jones.
p. cm. — (Step into reading. A step 1 book)
SUMMARY: Describes how bones perform different functions as part of the human body.
ISBN 0-679-89036-X (pbk.) — ISBN 0-679-99036-4 (lib. bdg.)
1. Bones—Juvenile literature. [1. Bones. 2. Skeleton.]
I. Jones, Davy, ill. II. Title. III. Series: Step into reading.
Step 1 book. QM101.K69 1999 611'.71—dc21 98-32041

Printed in the United States of America 10 9 8 7 6 5 4 3 2 1

Step into Reading®

BONES

By Stephen Krensky

Illustrated by Davy Jones

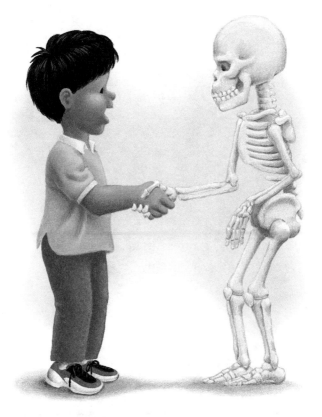

A Step 1 Book

Random House 🏠 New York

Walk.

Jump.

Touch your toes.

Bend your knees.
Hold your nose.

Any way you move,
your bones are helping out.

You have 206 bones
in your body.

These bones fit together
perfectly.
Together, they form
your *skeleton*.

Your bones are hidden
under your skin.

But you can feel them
and see their shape.

Your bones
start out small,
just the way you do.
As your bones grow,
you grow, too.

The smallest bones
are inside your ears.

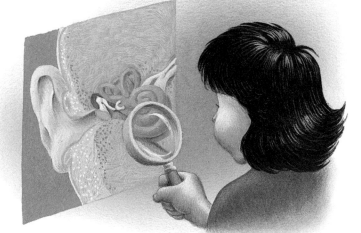

The biggest bones
are in your legs.

Some of your bones act as armor.

A flat bone in the middle of your chest protects your heart.

Your *ribs* are a bony cage

for your lungs

and other squishy parts.

The bones of your face
are part of your *skull*.
It covers your brain
like a helmet.

Some people think
skulls look scary.
They like
to wear skull masks
on Halloween.

Long ago,
pirates used a flag
with a skull and
crossbones on it
to frighten people.

Today, a skull
and crossbones means
danger or *poison*.
When you see it,
be careful!

Your bones do not bend.
So they are joined
in places where
you need to bend.
These places
are called *joints*.

Your *spine,*
or backbone,
has many joints.
It helps you
to stand up straight
or do a somersault.

Our bones work
with our *muscles*
to make our bodies move.

Bones are hard
and strong.
But sometimes they break
by accident.

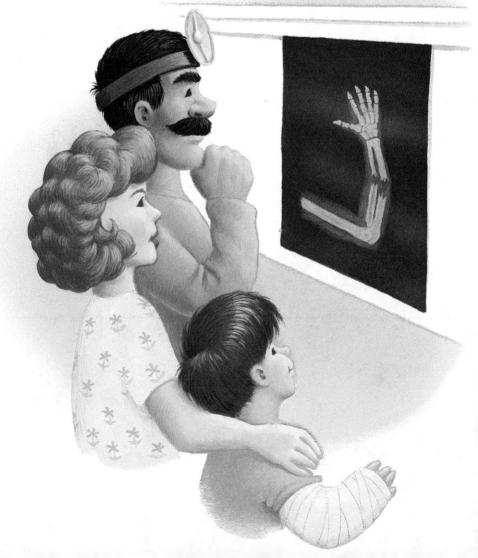

Luckily, the broken parts
can grow back together.
After many weeks,
the bone is healed.

Some old bones
turn into *fossils*
after millions of years.

Fossils tell us a lot
about animals
that lived long ago—
such as dinosaurs!

Many animals
have bones like ours.
But their skeletons match
their shapes and sizes.
Toads and goldfish have
much smaller bones
than we do.

Elephants and whales have
much bigger bones
than we do.

Some animals have
no bones at all.
Jellyfish and worms
wriggle and squiggle
without them.

If you had no bones,
you would look like a blob.

So when you run

or stretch

or grab

or chew,

think of your bones
and say, "Thank you!"

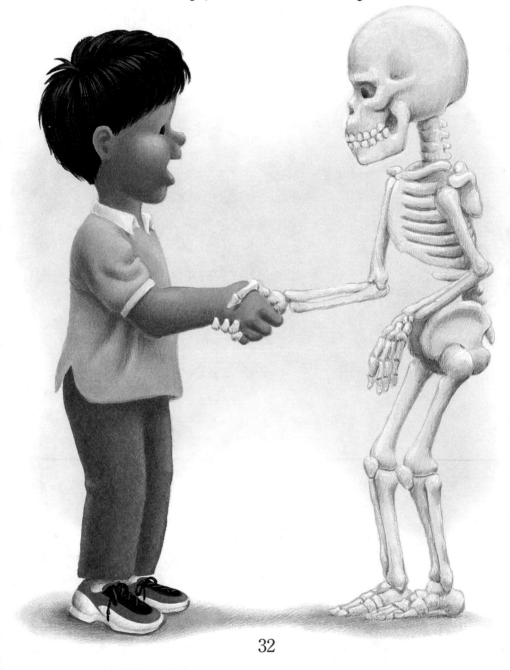